Published by Barbour Publishing, Inc., P. O. Box 719, Uhrichsville, Ohio 44683
http://www.barbourbooks.com

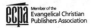 Member of the
Evangelical Christian
Publishers Association

Printed in China.

On Your Anniversary

ELLYN SANNA

BARBOUR
PUBLISHING, INC.

Happy Anniversary!

After all your years of marriage, you love your spouse more than you did in the beginning. Oh, life may have been more exciting back in your courtship days. Your heart may have pounded more often and your stomach flip-flopped every day with nervous exhilaration. But why would you trade the deeper love you have now for those more shallow thrills?

At the end of a long workday, the sound of your loved one's voice is sweeter than when you talked on the phone about your first date. The joy you find in your spouse's arms is far greater now than when you first kissed. And your friendship is more intimate than any you could have imagined when you were younger.

Having said all that, however, I have to add: Don't be surprised if now and then your heart still pounds and your stomach flip-flops.

Touchstones

∞

I need your love as a
touchstone of my existence.

JULIETTE DROUET TO VICTOR HUGO

Bright as Gold

A touchstone was once used to test gold; the metal left a streak on the stone that revealed the ore's purity. Over the years, that is how you may come to view your marriage: as a touchstone that reveals the relative worth of the other elements of your lives. Your relationship is the standard that helps you shape your priorities. It is the solid substance of your days—and against it, God's grace is revealed in your lives, shining bright as gold.

Mysterious is the fusion of two loving spirits: each takes the best from the other, but only to give it back again enriched with love.

ROMAIN ROLLAND

Your courageous gaiety has inspired me with joy. Your tender faithfulness has been a rock of security and comfort. I have felt for you all kinds of love at once. I have asked much of you and you have never failed me. You have intensified all colours, heightened all beauty, deepened all delight. I love you more than life, my beauty, my wonder.

DUFF COOPER (1890–1954), to his wife Diana

Joy is love exalted;
peace is love in repose;
long-suffering love is love enduring. . .
faith is love on the battlefield;
meekness is love in school;
and temperance is love in training.

DWIGHT L. MOODY (1837–1899)

Heaven itself descends in love;
A feeling from the Godhead caught,
To wean from self each sordid
thought;
A ray of Him who form'd the whole;
A glory circling round the soul!

BYRON

*When we reflect on the meaning of love,
we see that it is to the heart
what the summer is to the farmer's year.
It brings the harvest of all
the loveliest flowers of the soul.*

BILLY GRAHAM

An Endless Reflection

Do you remember having long, intense crushes when you were young? Month after month, you may have worshiped faithfully from afar, longing for a glance, a smile, a casual word of greeting. Each trivial exchange fed your one-sided infatuation. If you saw any reflection of God in your emotions, then He was a faraway God, a God you worshiped long-distance.

But married love gives you a very different image of God, for in marriage, you are loved even as you love; in marriage, you rejoice in each other's joy. Your love is reciprocal, intimate, and ever growing. Married love lends light to all the facets of your life—and the light that is reflected back only makes your love shine brighter still. Like a mirror that reflects a mirror, your love reaches into infinity.

Mutual love brings mutual delight.

R. H. DANA

Then I shall know fully,
even as I am fully known.

1 CORINTHIANS 13:12, NIV

A Dinner of Herbs

~

Better is a dinner of herbs where love is,
than a stalled ox and hatred therewith.

PROVERBS 15:17, KJV

True Riches

Well, yes, maybe you would like a bigger house—or perhaps you'd like to be able to travel more or buy a new car. And you'd love to be able to walk into your favorite store and buy whatever luxuries your heart desires, without ever stopping to worry about the grocery money.

But when you hear your spouse's car pull in the driveway at the end of the day, you know that none of that really matters at all. It truly is enough to live each day with your loved one, to share a home and a family and a life with the person you like best in all the world. All the little things—laughing together over your children's comments, talking over your day while you eat supper, waking up beside your spouse every morning—make you far richer than anything money could ever buy.

She is to her husband more than a friend. . .an equal with him in the yoke. Calamities and troubles she shares alike, nothing pleases her that doth not him. She is relative in all, and he without her is but half himself.

SIR THOMAS OVERBURY (1581–1613)

Levin asked himself again if
he really felt any regret for the freedom
his friends had been talking about.
The idea made him smile.
"Freedom? What do I need freedom for?
Happiness for me consists in loving. . . ."

LEO TOLSTOY, "ANNA KARENINA"

When one has fully entered the realm of love, the world—no matter how imperfect—becomes rich and beautiful, for it consists solely of opportunities for love.

SOREN KIERKEGAARD (1813–1855)

What Is a Wife?

The person who drives you crazy wanting to talk when you want to sleep, who cries for the most mysterious reasons, and yet still manages to be your best friend in all the world.

She's the only one who knows exactly how and where to scratch your back.

GERALD PARKINSON

[A wife is] magic.
Who else can mend
the television with a kick?

J. BATES

She's the person who rolls her eyes when you act like an adolescent, but loves you anyway.

What Is a Husband?

He is the household's official spider-remover and bee-killer.

The person who flirts with you on a "date" when you're dressed to the nines—and loves you just as much when you're exhausted, stringy-haired, and dressed in your sweats.

The person who can make you both happier and more exasperated than anyone else.

He is a business partner and a lover, sometimes an adversary, often a consultant, and always your biggest fan and truest friend.

Let the wife make her husband glad to come home
and let him make her sorry to see him leave.

MARTIN LUTHER (1483–1546)

Marriage is the life-long miracle,
The self-begetting wonder, daily fresh.

CHARLES KINGSELY

Duty does not have to be dull. Love can make it beautiful and fill it with life.

THOMAS MERTON

My Heart's Home

Sometimes after a fight you may go stomping out of the house, muttering insults under your breath, daydreaming about the days when you lived your life the way you wanted, without always having to compromise with another person. But all you need to do is walk down to the corner and back, and by then you'll usually realize how glad, how grateful, how blessed you are to be married to the one you love.

A life that was all yours, not shared, would be a colder, poorer life. It would lack all the wonder and unexpected riches your spouse has poured into your heart. It would be bare and sterile and lonely.

Your marriage is your home, the place where you are secure and comfortable and loved.

The married are those who have taken the terrible risk of intimacy and, having taken it, know life without intimacy to be impossible.

CAROLYN HEILBRUN

Love comforteth,
like sunshine after rain. . .
Love's gentle spring
doth always fresh remain.

WILLIAM SHAKESPEARE

Love's Journey

*Marriage is not a state, but a movement—
a boundless adventure.*

PAUL TOURNIER

The Journey

The young woman tucked a small package between two sweaters and closed the suitcase. "I'm ready," she said and handed the suitcase to her husband. She opened the car door and slid onto the passenger seat, while her husband unlocked the trunk and placed their suitcase next to a gift-wrapped box.

Headed down the highway, they passed piles of wet, matted-down leaves. Silver maple trees with bare limbs swayed in the wind. She turned on the heater and covered her lap with a fleece blanket.

"Our beautiful autumn is all gone," she said.

He nodded. "Look up there." As they climbed higher, the tops of the pine trees were sprinkled with white powder.

"The season's first snowfall," she said. "It's like a whole other world."

They traveled south across the state border, and the snow disappeared. When they finally reached the inn, they found the entrance lined with hardy orange and yellow mums.

"The grass is still green here," she commented.

Later, they strolled hand in hand through the woods. After he carved their initials in a white birch, he picked up the shavings and put them in his back pocket.

After dinner, she handed him the small package. He tore the wrapping paper and then read the title on the cassette: "Our Wedding."

"Here's your gift," he said.

She slipped the lid off the gift-wrapped box and smiled. "You made us a scrapbook."

"I tried to capture the milestones of our journey together so far," he said.

"I love you." She leaned close and kissed him.

As they snuggled, shadows danced in the candlelight. They listened to the recording of their wedding ceremony that she had given him, and then they looked through the scrapbook he had made.

Together they decorated another page in the scrapbook. She wrote "Our First Anniversary" on a piece of stationery with the inn's letterhead. He added shavings from the birch tree.

After that, every year when the last leaves fell from the trees, they traveled somewhere together. No matter their destination, their luggage always contained two gifts. They adventured as far as Barbados and as near as the local bed and breakfast. Some years they had to stay home because they were waiting for a baby, but on their anniversary they still packed two gifts in a suitcase.

And each year they snuggled as shadows danced in the candlelight. They opened the suitcase and exchanged the same two gifts: a small package and a gift-wrapped box. As they listened to the recording of their wedding ceremony, they looked through the scrapbook and traveled again along the journey of their marriage. Sometimes the journey led past bare, cold trees, through glittering snow—but always, sooner or later, they would find a place where the grass was still green and hardy mums lined their path with brilliant color.

DONNA LANGE

have lived long enough to know that the evening glow of love has its own riches and splendour.

BENJAMIN DISRAELI

'Tis you alone that sweetens life,
and makes one wish the wings of time were clipt,
which not only seems but really flies away too fast,
much too fast, for those that love. . . .

JOHN HERVEY, TO HIS WIFE ELIZABETH

23

*A happy marriage is
the union of two good forgivers.*

ROBERT QUILLEN

My love, I've found that the only way to travel further on our journey is to be always willing to forgive. Thank you for all the times you forgive me each and every day. Thank you for making real to me the even greater forgiveness of Christ.

*A successful marriage is an edifice
that must be rebuilt every day.*

ANDRÈ MAUROIS

Stitched Together by Love

There are many jokes that refer to marriage as a ball and chain. However, you and your spouse are not captives; your hearts are not trapped, longing for personal freedom.

Instead, you have given yourselves to each other freely, by choice—and each day you make that choice anew, moment by moment. It is all of those moments of commitment, those tiny stitches of love you each choose to make, that tie your hearts together forever.

Chains do not hold a marriage together.
It is threads, hundreds of tiny threads that
sew people together through the years.

SIMONE SIGNORET

The Heart's Friend

Fair is the white star of twilight,
And the moon roving
To the sky's end;
But she is fairer, better worth loving,
She, my heart's friend.

SHOSHONE LOVE SONG

True Intimacy

You probably have plenty of same-gender friends, people who think the way you do, who understand exactly what you mean without any lengthy explanations. Meanwhile, the way your spouse's mind works is often a mystery to you. You can explain yourself until you're blue in the face, and sometimes your loved one never quite grasps what you're trying to say. You're on entirely different wavelengths.

But for all that, you are each the other's deepest and truest friend; you are friends who know and love each other unconditionally. If you thought just alike, your friendship might be less frustrating, but it would also be far less interesting.

You would hate to lose your other friends. But your friendship with your partner, a friendship built on commitment, on a shared life, on an intimacy that goes far deeper than simply thinking the same way, that friendship is more infinitely precious than any other. Through all life's changing seasons, you are very best friends—forever friends.

How much the wife is dearer than the bride.

GEORGE LYTTLETON (1719–1773)

There is no happy life
But in a wife;
The comforts are so sweet
When they do meet:
'Tis plenty, peace, a calm
Like dropping balm. . . .

WILLIAM CAVENDISH
(1592–1676)

When a man. . . .is happily, blissfully married, the scope of his reflections is necessarily limited. . . . He is no longer haunted by the face of every pretty girl he meets, for he has already met the woman most fitted in the wide world to make him happy. . . . He is no longer prone to dreams about the object of his affections, for he has her perpetually beside him.

ROBERT GRANT,
Reflections of a Married Man (1892)

*Love is mutual self-giving
that ends in self-recovery.*

FULTON J. SHEEN

29

My Wife

Trusty, dusky, vivid, true,
With eyes of gold and bramble-dew,
Steel true and blade-straight,
The great Artificer
Made my mate.

Teacher, tender, comrade, wife,
A fellow-farer true through life,
Heart-whole and soul-free,
The august Father
Gave to me.

ROBERT LOUIS STEVENSON
(1850–1894)

What is there in the vale of life
Half so delightful as a wife,
When friendship, love, and peace combine
To stamp the marriage-bond divine?
WILLIAM COWPER (1731–1800)

*Love is the expansion of two natures
in such a fashion that each includes the other,
each is enriched by the other.*

FELIX ADLER

Love Ever Grows

*I bless you. I kiss and caress. . .
and gaze into your deep,
sweet eyes which long ago
conquered me completely.
Love ever grows.*

**TSARITSA ALEXANDRA (1872–1918),
TO TSAR NICHOLAS II**

Worth It All

Be glad you both took your marriage vows seriously. If you hadn't, there would have been times when you could have walked away from each other. Marriage wasn't fun those times; walking out on your promises would have been far easier.

But if you had, think what you would have missed: all the laughter and tenderness and joy that came after those bad spots. No, your relationship isn't always easy. But you can always rely on the fact that the hard times never last forever—and the love that grows even in the midst of pain is worth the effort.

I do love you. . .as the dew loves the flowers; as the birds love the sunshine; as the wavelets love the breeze; as mothers love their firstborn; as memory loves old faces; as the yearning tides love the moon; as angels love the pure in heart.

MARK TWAIN (1835–1910)

She gave me eyes, she gave me ears;
And humble cares, and delicate fears;
A heart, the fountain of sweet tears;
And love, and thought, and joy.

WILLIAM WORDSWORTH (1770–1850)

A Lifetime of Riches

Why is it that people find weddings so fascinating? That one day involves so much planning and excitement. Everyone celebrates with the happy couple.

And of course, none of us begrudge the newlyweds all the attention. But really, don't you think people should be even more excited by the fact that the two of you have been married all this time? Shouldn't everyone celebrate the fact that your marriage grows richer and deeper day by day? A wedding takes just an hour or so, but a marriage takes a lifetime.

There is no applause in marriage.
No one applauds a flowering tree.

HAROLD PHILIPS

35

A good husband makes a good wife. . .
AND a good wife makes a good husband.

PROVERB

*I*f twenty years were to be erased and I were to be pre-
sented with the same choice again under the same cir-
cumstances I would act precisely as I did then. . . . I
have needed her all these twenty years. I love her and I
need her now. I always will.

THE DUKE OF WINDSOR, about his wife

A successful marriage demands a divorce:
a divorce from your self-love.

PAUL FROST

A successful marriage is not a gift;
it is an achievement.

ANN LANDERS

The Christian is supposed to love his neighbor, and since his wife is his nearest neighbor, she should be his deepest love.

MARTIN LUTHER (1483–1546)

Forgetting oneself is not a refinement of love.
It is a first condition of love.

LEON JOSEPH SUENENS

Love does not dominate; it cultivates.

**JOHANN WOLFGANG VON GOETHE
(1749–1832)**

Love is like friendship caught on fire. In the beginning a flame, very pretty, often hot and fierce but still only light and flickering. As love grows older, our hearts mature and our lives become as coals, deep-burning and unquenchable.

BRUCE LEE

Love spends all, and still hath store.

PHILIP JAMES BAILEY

The essential nature of marriage consists in a certain indivisible union of minds by which each one of the consorts is bound to keep inviolably his faith with the other.

THOMAS AQUINAS (13th century)

Between a man and his wife
nothing ought to rule but love.

WILLIAM PENN (17TH CENTURY)

Love isn't like a reservoir. You'll never drain it dry. It's much more like a natural spring. The longer and the farther it flows, the stronger and deeper and the clearer it becomes.

EDDIE CANTOR

A Reflection of God's Love

Remember what it was like to go out on dates, the excitement of first attraction, the anticipation of that first embrace? As wonderful as those moments were, wouldn't you rather have the sure knowledge of your spouse's constant love, the security of your lifelong faithfulness? These days you don't have to agonize and obsess and dream about your relationship; instead, you can simply walk out on its bedrock, knowing it will hold your weight, for it is the solid foundation from which your lives grow.

And that is why, on your anniversary and always, the two of you together are an image of God's unfailing love.

Love and faithfulness always breed confidence.

FRANCIS DE SALES